OFF-TO-COLLEGE

COOKBOOK

by Barb Layton

This book, as is true of all our cookbooks,
is available to organizations as a fundraise
Easy Terms ...... High Returns

i

Hearts & Tummies Cookbook Co.
Division of **Quixote Press**
Bruce Carlson, Publisher

Printed in U.S.A.

Yes, there is life after pizza, fries, 'n' burgers.
And the good-for-you goodies you can cook up from
these recipes would make Mom proud.

This is cooking that makes it easy to get in
& get out of the cookin' business of an evening
when there are more important things to get to.

Table of Contents

Soups

Broccoli and Shrimp Chowder

1 c. milk
1/8 tsp garlic powder
1/8 tsp dried thyme
  leaves
1 (10 oz) pkg frozen
  cut broccoli in
  cheese -flavored
  sauce

1/3 c. chopped
  tomato
1 c. (4 oz) frozen,
  cleaned, uncooked
  shrimp

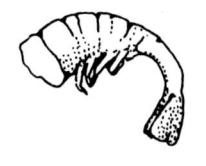

In saucepan, combine milk, garlic powder, thyme & broccoli. Cook over medium heat until hot & bubbly, stirring occasionally. Gently stir in tomato & shrimp; cook until shrimp are opaque.

Light & Easy
Cauliflower Soup

1/4 large head
 cauliflower, separated
 into flowerets, sliced
1/2 medium onion,
 sliced
1-1/2 c water

1-2 vegetable
 bouillon cubes
1/4 tsp salt
1/4 c nonfat dry milk
 powder
2 0z Cheddar cheese
 shredded

Combine cauliflower, onion, water, bouillon & salt in saucepan; heat over medium heat to boiling. Reduce heat; simmer, covered, until cauliflower is tender, about 15 minutes. Stir in dry milk powder. Add cheese; cook & stir until cheese is melted. Serve as is, or process in blender until smooth.

Fresh Spinach Soup

1/2 Tbsp margarine
1 c. loosely- packed
  chopped spinach
  leaves
1/2 can cream of
  potato soup

1/2 soup can milk
1 Tbsp dry sherry
  or vermouth
dash of nutmeg

In microwave-safe casserole, combine margarine & spinach. Cover with lid; microwave on High 2 minutes or until spinach is wilted. Stir in soup until smooth; stir in milk, sherry & nutmeg until well-blended. Cover; microwave on High 6 minutes or until hot & bubbling, stirring once during cooking.

8

Chunky Tomato Vegetable Soup

1/2 can tomato soup
3/4 c. water
1/2 tomato,
  coarsely chopped
1/2 green pepper,
  coarsely chopped
1/2 zucchini,
  coarsely chopped

1/4 tsp beef-flavored
  instant bouillon
1/4 tsp basil leaves
  crushed
1/8 tsp Worcestershire
  sauce

In saucepan, combine all ingredients. Bring to a boil. Reduce heat; cover & simmer 3-5 minutes, stirring occasionally. Serve immediately.

Tomato-French Onion Soup

1/2 can tomato soup
1/2 can French
  onion soup
1 soup can, water

toasted bread slices,
  quartered or croutons
grated Parmesan
  cheese

Heat soups & water. Serve in bowls topped with bread & sprinkled with cheese.

Cheese & Beer Soup

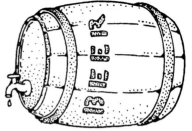

1 Tbsp margarine
1 Tbsp flour
1/2 pkg. dry onion
  soup mix
1-1/2 c. milk
1/2 tsp Worcestershire
  sauce

1/2 c. Cheddar
  cheese,
  shredded
1/4 c. beer
1/2 tsp prepared
  mustard

In saucepn, melt butter & cook flour over medium heat, stirring constantly, 3 min. or til bubbling. Stir in soup mix that has been blended with milk & Worcestershire sauce. Bring just to boiling point, then simmer, stirring occasionally, 10 min. Stir in remaining ingredients & simmer, stirring constantly, 5 min. or until cheese is melted. Garnish, if desired, with additional cheese, chopped red pepper & parsley.

Chowdery Cheese Soup

3 slices bacon
2 Tbsp onion, chopped
1 Tbsp flour
1/8 tsp dry mustard
dash pepper
1/2 tsp Worcestershire sauce
1-1/2 c. milk
1 c. shredded American cheese

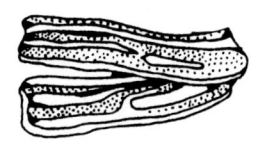

In saucepan, cook bacon til crisp. Remove bacon from pan; drain, reserving 1 Tbsp of drippings in pan. Crumble bacon; set aside. Saute onion in drippings til tender. Blend in flour, mustard, pepper, & Worcestershire sauce; gradually add milk, stirring constantly. Cook til slightly thickened, about 10 minutes. Stir in cheese & bacon. Cook over low heat til cheese is melted, stirring occasionally. Serve hot.

Quick & Easy Stew

1/4 c. flour
3/4 lb. round steak, cut
  in 2" cubes or stew
  meat
1 onion, quartered
1/2 can tomato soup

1/4 of soup can
  water,(about
  1/4 c.)
season to taste
with favorite
seasonings

Coat meat with flour. Combine all ingredients in greased casserole
dish. Cover & bake at 350° for 1 hour.

Quick & Easy Stroganoff Soup

1/2 can cream of mushroom soup
11/2 can beef noodle soup
3/4 c. water
1/4 c. cubed, cooked beef
1/4 tsp paprika

2 Tbsp sour cream
1-1/2 tsp dry sherry, if desired

In saucepan, combine soups, water, beef, & paprika. Bring to a boil, stirring frequently. Reduce heat; stir in sour cream & sherry. Heat gently, stirring frequently. Do not boil.

Salads & Dips

15

Apple & Grape Salad

1/2 c. cubed apples
1/4 c. seedless grape halves
2 Tbsp chopped celery
1/4 tsp lemon juice
about 1/4 c. mayonnaise

Combine all ingredients. Mix lightly; chill.
Serve in lettuce-lined bowl, if desired.

Carrot-Raisin Salad

2 c. coarsely shredded carrot
1/4 c. raisins
1-1/2 Tbsp mayonnaise
4 oz unsweetened crushed pineapple,
  undrained

Combine all ingredients in a bowl; toss well. Cover & chill 1 hour.

Pistachio Salad

9 oz. whipped topping
1 box instant pistachio
  pudding
1 lb. can crushed pine-
  apple & juice

1 c. miniature
  marshmallows
1/2 c. nuts

Fold dry pudding mix into whipped topping. Add pineapple, juice, marshmallows, and nuts. Refrigerate.

Vegetable Dip

4 oz. cream cheese,
  softened
1/4 c. plain yogurt
1 Tbsp milk
5 oz. frozen spinach,
  thawed, well-drained,
  chopped

1 hard-cooked egg,
  finely chopped
1/8 tsp salt
1/8 tsp pepper

Combine cream cheese, yogurt, & milk; mixing until well-blended.
Stir in remaining ingredients. Serve with cut-up vegetables.

Dilled Garden Dip

1-1/2 c. (12 oz.) lowfat
  cottage cheese
2 Tbsp lemon juice
2 Tbsp shredded carrot
1 Tbsp sliced green
  onions

1 Tbsp chopped
  parsley
1/1-2 tsp chopped
  fresh dill or
  1/2 tsp dill weed
dash pepper

In blender, combine cottage cheese & lemon juice. Blend 3-5 minutes
at medium speed or until smooth. Stir in remaining ingredients.
Serve with cut-up fresh vegetables for dipping or as a topping for
baked potatoes.

Mexicali Dip

4 oz. cream cheese, softened
3/4 c. dairy sour cream
1/2 of a 1.25 oz. pkg taco seasoning mix

In small bowl, combine all ingredients; beat until smooth & creamy.
Cover; refrigerate several hours to blend flavors.
Serve with tortilla chips or assorted raw vegetable dippers.

Sausage-Cheese Dip

1/2 lb. ground beef
1/2 lb. bulk pork sausage
1/2 onion, minced
1 lb. Velveeta cheese
1/2 tsp garlic powder

3-3/4 oz Jalapeno
relish or green
chilies
1/2 can cream of
mushroom soup

Cook ground beef, sausage & onion together. Drain well. Add chunks of cheese & stir over low heat until melted. Add remaining ingredients. Serve hot with corn chips. Freezes well. Can also cook in a crock pot on low for 1-2 hours; stirring occasionally.

Guacamole

1 ripe avocado, peeled, mashed
2 Tbsp mayonnaise
1-1/2 Tbsp lemon juice
2-4 drops hot pepper
  sauce
1/8 tsp salt
dash pepper

In small bowl, combine all ingredients until smooth. Cover;
refrigerate 1-2 hours to blend flavors.

My Favorite Recipes

Pasta & Misc.

One-Pan Macaroni & Cheese

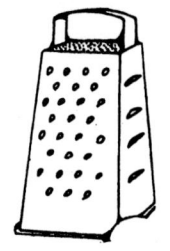

1 c. macaroni, cooked & drained
1/4 c. water
1/2 c. instant nonfat dry milk (or 1/3 c. non-
  instant
1/2 c. process cheese, cut-up

Mix water & dry milk. Add to macaroni in pan. Add cheese & cook over
low heat & stir until cheese melts. Let stand a few minutes for a thicker
sauce, or add a little water for a thinner sauce.

Yankee Noodle Bake

4 hot dogs, cut in 1/2"
   pieces
2 Tbsp onion, chopped
1 Tbsp margarine
1/2 can tomato soup
1/4 c. water

1/2 tsp prepared
   mustard
1 c. cooked noodles
1 Tbsp buttered
   bread crumbs

In saucepan, brown hot dogs & cook onion in margarine until tender.
Stir in remaining ingredients except crumbs. Pour into 1 qt.
casserole. Bake at 350° for 25 minutes or until hot; stir. Top with
crumbs. Bake 5 minutes longer.

Creamy Fettucini Alfredo

4 oz. cream cheese, cubed
1/3 c. grated Parmesan cheese
1/4 c. margarine
1/4 c. milk
4 oz. fettucini, cooked and drained

In saucepan, combine all ingredients, except fettucini. Stir over low heat until smooth. Add fettucini; toss lightly.

Golden Tomato Rabbit

1 or 2 slices bacon
1/2 onion, chopped
1/2 can tomato soup
2 Tbsp milk
1/2 c. shredded, sharp process cheese
toast

In saucepan, cook bacon until crisp; remove & crumble. Cook onion in drippings until tender. Blend in soup, milk & cheese. Heat until cheese melts; stir occasionally. Serve over toast; garnish with bacon.

Creamy Tortellini Primavera

1-1/2 Tbsp olive or vegetable oil & 1/2 clove garlic, minced

1/2 lb. egg or spinach tortellini, cooked & drained

1/2 envelope dry vegetable recipe soup mix

1/8 tsp pepper

1 c. light cream or half & half

2 Tbsp grated Parmesan cheese

2 Tbsp finely chopped parsley

In large skillet, heat oil & cook garlic until golden. Stir in cooked tortellini, then vegetable recipe soup mix blended with cream. Bring to the boiling point, then simmer, stirring occasionally, 5 minutes. Stir in remaining ingredients. Garnish, if desired, with additional parsley & cheese. These are great appetizers.

Cottage Cheese Pancakes

1/4 lb. cottage cheese	1-1/2 Tbsp sour
1 egg	cream
1/8 tsp salt	1/3 c. flour
1 Tbsp sugar	

Mix all ingredients together. Place a heaping tablespoon of batter on a hot greased griddle & brown both sides.
Serve with your favorite topping.

My Favorite Recipes

Ground Beef

Meat Loaf

1 lb. ground beef
1 c. cracker crumbs
1 egg plus milk to
   make 1 cup liquid

1 tsp salt
1 Tbsp dried onion
   or 1 small onion

Form in loaf & chill. Bake covered with foil for 30 minutes at 350°.
Uncover & spread with catsup & bake for 30 miutes longer. Can substitute the following piquant sauce for catsup: 1/4 c. catsup, 1/4 c. nutmeg, 3 Tbsp brown sugar, 1 tsp dry mustard. Mix all together.

Meat Loaf

4 slices process American cheese
1 lb ground beef
3/4 c. dry bread crumbs
1/3 c. catsup
1 egg
1/2 pkg. dry onion soup mix

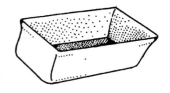

Cut 3 slices cheese into small pieces; combine with remaining ingredients. Mix well. In shallow baking pan, shape into loaf. Bake 1 hour at 350° (325° for glass dish). Remove from oven; arrange remaining cheese slice on top. Return to oven 5 minutes more or until cheese begins to melt.

Chili Dogs

1/4 lb. ground beef
1/8 tsp salt
1/8 c. water
1/8 c. onion,
 chopped

1/8 tsp garlic
 clove, minced
1/2 can tomato
 sauce (4 oz.)
1/4 tsp chili powder

Cook ground beef; drain. Add remaining ingredients & simmer for 10 minutes.

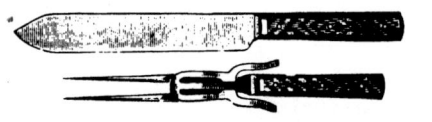

Sloppy Joes

1/2 lb. ground beef
1/4 c. chopped onion
1/4 c. chopped green
 pepper
1/2 c. ketchup
1/8 c. water

1 tsp beef flavor
 bouillon granules
 (or 1 cube)
1 tsp sugar
1/2 tsp prepared
 mustard

In skillet brown beef with onion & **pepper**; drain. Add remaining
ingredients, bring to a boil. Reduce heat; cover & simmer 15 minutes.
Serve on hamburger buns.

Cheesy Sloppy Joes

1/2 lb. ground beef
1/4 c. celery, chopped
1/4 c. onion, chopped
1/2 c. (4 oz.) pasteurized,
  processed cheese spread

1 Tbsp catsup
1/2 Tbsp Worcester-
  shire sauce

Brown beef, celery, & onion; drain. Add cheese spread, catsup, & Worcestershire sauce. Cook slowly until mixture is smooth. Serve on hamburger buns.

Tempting Taco Burgers

1/2 envelope dry onion soup mix (or onion-mushroom or beefy onion)
1/2 lb. ground beef
1/4 c. chopped tomato

2 T. finely chopped green pepper
1/2 tsp chili powder
2 T. water

In large bowl, combine all ingredients; shape into 2 patties. Grill, broil, or fry until done. Serve, if desired, on hamburger buns & top with shredded lettuce & Cheddar cheese.

Tomato Beef Casserole

1/2 lb. ground beef
1/4 c. onion, chopped
1/2 c. shredded
  Cheddar cheese
1/2 can tomato soup

1 c. cooked medium
  noodles
1/2 c. cooked corn
2 Tbsp water
1/4 tsp salt

In saucepan, brown beef & cook onion until tender; drain. Stir in 1/4 cup cheese & remaining ingredients. Pour into 1 qt. casserole. Bake at 350° for 30 minutes or until hot; stir. Top with remaining cheese.

Beefy Noodle Skillet

1/2 lb. ground beef
7 oz. meatless spaghetti sauce
2 oz. (1 cup) uncooked medium egg noodles
1/4 c. sliced ripe olives
3/4 c. water
1/4 tsp dried oregano leaves
1/4 tsp instant minced garlic
1/4 c. shredded Cheddar cheese

Cook ground beef in skillet, stirring frequently, until brown; drain. Stir in remaining ingredients except cheese. Heat to boiling; reduce heat. Cover & simmer about 15 min. or until noodles are tender. Stir in cheese. Cover & simmer 5 min.

Skillet Beef & Egg Noodles

1/2 lb. ground beef
1/2 envelope dry onion soup mix
14 oz. whole canned tomatoes, undrained

4 oz. can whole kernel corn, undrained
2 oz. (1 c.) uncooked egg noodles

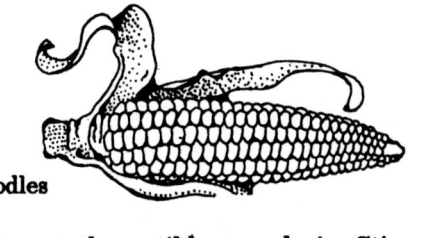

Cook ground beef in skillet, stirring frequently, until brown; drain. Stir in remaining ingredients; breaking up the tomatoes. Heat to boiling; reduce heat. Cover & simmer about 20 minutes, stirring occasionally, until noodles are tender.

Stroganoff Skillet

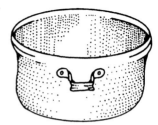

1/2 ground beef
1/2 onion, chopped
1/2 can cream of mush-
   room soup
1/2 can beef broth

1/2 c. (4 oz.) sour
   cream
1/4 c. water
1-1/2 c. uncooked
   egg noodles

Brown ground beef & onion; drain. Blend in mushroom soup & sour cream; add remaining ingredients. Bring to a boil, then reduce heat. Cover, cook 10 minutes or until noodles are done. Stir often.

Hamburger-Cottage Cheese Casserole

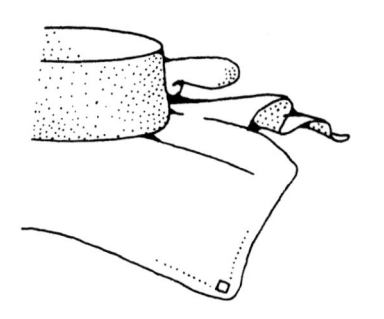

1/2 lb. ground beef
1/2 onion, chopped
1/2 pkg. egg noodles
1 c. (8 oz.)
  cottage cheese

1/2 c. sour cream
salt & pepper
  to taste

Brown beef & onion; drain. Miss all ingredients in a 1 qt. casserole.
Sprinkle with paprika. Bake at 300° for 20-30 minutes.

Spanish Noodles

1/2 lb. ground beef
8 oz. wide noodles,
  cooked
1/2 green pepper,
  chopped
1/2 can cream style
  corn

8 oz. tomato sauce
1/2 can ripe olives,
  chopped
1/2 c. shredded
  Cheddar cheese

Brown beef; drain. Combine with remaining ingredients, except for cheese. Top with cheese & bake 1 hour at 325°.

Beef Nacho Casserole

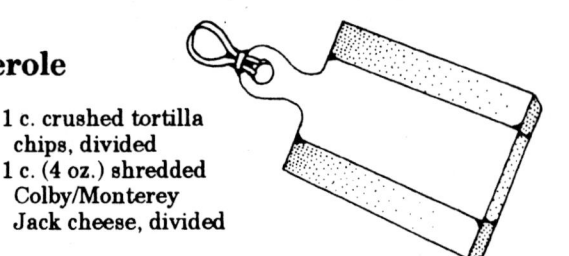

1/2 lb. ground beef
6 oz. chunky salsa
1/2 c. sweet corn
1/2 c. mayonnaise
1-1/2 tsp chili powder

1 c. crushed tortilla chips, divided
1 c. (4 oz.) shredded Colby/Monterey Jack cheese, divided

Heat oven to 350°. brown beef; drain. Stir in salsa, corn, mayonnaise & chili powder. Layer 1/2 each of the meat mixture, chips, & cheese in a 1 qt. casserole. Repeat layers. Bake 20 minutes or until thoroughly heated. Top with shredded lettuce & chopped tomato, if desired.

46

Pizza Cups

3/4 lb. ground beef
1 can (6 oz.) tomato paste
1 Tbsp instant minced
  onion
1 tsp Italian seasoning

1/2 tsp salt
1 can (10 oz.) re-
  frigerated biscuits
1/2-3/4 c. shredded
  mozzarella cheese

Brown & drain beef. Stir in tomato paste, onion, & seasonings (mixture will be thick). Cook over low heat for 5 minutes, stirring frequently. Place biscuits in a greased muffin tin, pressing to cover bottom & sides. Spoon about 1/4 c. of meat mixture into biscuit-lined cups & sprinkle with cheese. Bake at 400° for 12 minutes or until golden brown.
Yield: 12

Pizza Noodle Bake

1/2 lb. ground beef
1/4 c. onion, chopped
7-1/2 oz. tomato sauce
3/4 c. water
1/4 tsp oregano
1 tsp basil leaves

1/8 tsp garlic powder
1-1/2 c. uncooked
  egg noodles
1 c. mozzarella
  cheese, shredded

Cook the beef & onion; drain. Mix the sauce, water, & seasonings together. Put the sauce mixture, beef, & noodles in a 9x9" pan or casserole; mix together & bake at 350° for 1 hour. The last 10 minutes, sprinkle the cheese over the top.

Lasagna Toss

1/2 lb. ground beef
1/4 c. chopped onion
dash minced garlic
1/4 tsp salt
1 c. spaghetti sauce

3 oz. spiral noodles,
    cooked & drained
1/2 c. cottage cheese
1 c. shredded Moz-
    zarella cheese div.

Brown beef, onion, garlic, & salt. Stir in spaghetti sauce, simmer until heated. Remove 1/2 cup of meat sauce; set aside. Stir noodles into the remaining sauce. Place half of noodle-sauce mixture in greased 1-1/2 quart casserole. Cover with cottage cheese & 1/2 cup Mozzarella cheese. Add remaining noodle-sauce mixture; top with the 1/2 cup of reserved meat sauce & remaining Mozzarella cheese. Sprinkle with Parmesan cheese. Cover & bake at 350° for 20-25 minutes. Let stand 5 minutes before serving.

Lasagne with Uncooked Noodles

1-1/2 c. water
2 jars (15 oz. ea.) spaghetti sauce/mushrooms
1 (16 oz.) box lasagne noodles
1 (15 oz.) container cottage cheese

1-2 eggs
8 oz. mozzarella cheese, shredded
1/2 c. grated parmesan cheese

Mix water & spaghetti sauce in measuring bowl. Pour 1-1/2 c. sauce in bottom of 9x13x2" pan. Arrange layer of uncooked noodles, slightly overlapping. Spread 1/2 cottage cheese that has been mixed with egg, over noodles. Spread 1/2 mozzarella cheese over cottage cheese. Sprinkle with 2 Tbsp parmesan cheese. Add another layer of sauce (1-1/2 c.) Repeat with another layer of noodles, remaining mixtures of cottage cheese, mozzarella & 2 Tbsp parmesan cheese. Top with layer of noodles and remaining sauce. Sprinkle with rest of parmesan cheese. Cover tightly with heavy-duty aluminum foil. Set on cookie sheet & bake for 1 hour at 350°, or until knife passes easily thru pasta. Let stand covered on rack for 10 min. & cut into servings.

One-Pot Spaghetti

1/2 lb. ground beef
3-1/2 oz. spaghetti
7 oz. spaghetti sauce
  with mushrooms
4 oz. tomato sauce
1 c. water

1 Tbsp instant
  minced onion
1/2 tsp sugar
grated Parmesan
  cheese, if desired

Cook ground beef in Dutch oven, stirring frequently, until brown;
drain. Break spaghetti in half. Stir spaghetti & remaining
ingredients except cheese into beef. Heat to boiling over medium-high
heat, stirring occasionally; reduce heat. Cover & simmer over low
heat about 15 minutes or until **spaghetti** is tender. Stir; sprinkle with
cheese.

51

Quick & Easy Tacos

1/2 lb. ground beef
1/2 can whole peeled
tomatoes, drained &
coarsely chopped
(reserve liquid)
1/2 green pepper,
finely chopped
4 taco shells

1/2 env. dry onion
soup mix (or onion-
mushroom or beefy
mushroom)
1-1/2 tsp chili powder
1-2 drops hot pepper
sauce
taco toppings*

In medium skillet, brown beef; drain. Stir in tomatoes, green pepper, then soup mix blended with reserved liquid, chili powder, & hot pepper sauce. Bring to a boil, then simmer 15 minutes or til slightly thickened. Serve in taco shells with assorted taco toppings. *Taco toppings: use shredded Cheddar or Monterey Jack cheese, shredded lettuce, chopped tomatoes, sour cream or taco sauce.

Chop-Chop Chow Mein

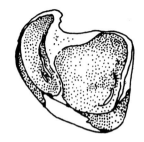

1/2 lb. ground beef
1/2 onion, chopped
1-2 stalks celery, sliced
2 Tbsp flour
1 Tbsp soy sauce
1 c. water
1 tsp beef bouillon
  granuels

1/2 can (1 cup) bean
  sprouts, drained
1/2 can (2 oz.) mush-
  room pieces &
  stems, undrained

In skillet, brown meat & cook onion & celery until tender; drain. Stir in flour. Add remaining ingredients. Heat to boiling, stirring constantly. Simmer 10-15 minutes. Serve over rice if desired.

Sausage Casserole

1/2 lb. sausage, cooked & drained
1/2 c. rice
1 c. celery, chopped
1/2 c. onion, chopped

1/4 c. green pepper, chopped
1/2 can cream of chicken soup

Cook rice. Cook next 4 ingredients together for 6 minutes. Combine all ingredients & bake 35-40 minutes at 350°.

Meats

Grilled Steak with Mushroom - Wine Sauce

2 steaks, cut 1" thick
1-1/2 Tbsp margarine
1/4 lb (about 1 c.) mush-
  rooms, sliced
2 Tbsp white wine
1 Tbsp minced parsley
1/4 tsp dried tarra-
  gon, crushed
1/2 tsp instant
  beef bouillon
  granules

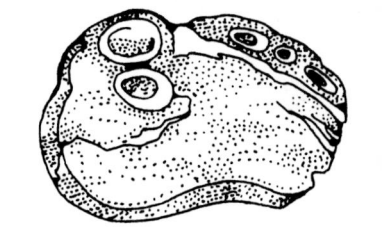

Slash any fat around edge of steaks every 4 inches. Grill steaks to desired doneness. While steak is grilling, heat margarine in skillet until hot. Add mushrooms & saute 1 minute or until tender. Add remaining ingredients & simmer 4 minutes, stirring often. Serve sauce over steak.

Steak Orientale

1/4 c. Wish-bone Italian dressing
1 Tbsp soy sauce
1/2 Tbsp brown sugar
1/2 lb. steak
green pepper, cut into chunks (about 1/4 pepper)
1/2 onion, sliced

In shallow baking dish, blend dressing, soy sauce, & brown sugar; add beef, green pepper, & onion. Cover & marinate in refrigerator, turning occasionally, 4 hours or overnight. Remove beef & vegetables, reserving marinade. Broil steak, turning & basting frequently with reserved marinade, until done. During the last 20 minutes of cooking, add vegetables.

Beef Stroganoff

1/2 lb. boneless beef
  sirloin steak
1/4 c. onion, chopped
1/4 c. sour cream
1/4 tsp paprika
Hot cooked noodles

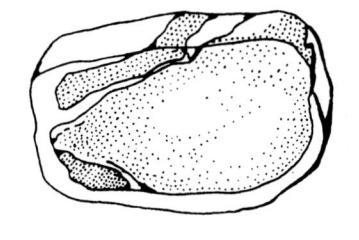

Freeze steak 1 hour to make slicing easier. Cut steak into very thin slices across the grain. In microwave-safe casserole, combine beef & onion. Cover with lid; microwave on High 5 minutes or until beef is no longer pink, stirring once during cooking. In small bowl, stir soup until smooth; stir in sour cream & paprika. Add beef, stirring to coat. Cover; microwave at 50% power 3 minutes or until heated through. Serve over noodles.

58

Burgundy Beef

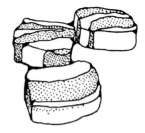

1/2 lb. sirloin steak, cut into 1 inch pieces
1 Tbsp margarine
8 oz. frozen vegetable combination (zucchini, cauliflower & carrots)

1/2 can beef gravy
2 Tbsp tomato paste
2 Tbsp burgundy or dry red wine
1/8 tsp garlic powder

In skillet cook beef in margarine until beef is browned. Remove beef from skillet. Combine remaining ingredients in the skillet & heat to boiling. Return beef to skillet & reduce heat to low. Cover; cook 10 minutes or until vegetables are tender.
Serve over rice.

Stroganoff Supreme

3/4 lb. thinly sliced
  round steak
salt & pepper
  to taste
2 Tbsp margarine

1/2 can beef broth
1/4 c. water
1-1/2 Tbsp flour
1/4 c. sour cream

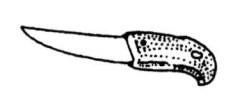

Cut beef into thin strips; sprinkle with seasonings. Brown in
margarine in skillet. Add broth. Cover; simmer 1 hour. Gradually
blend water into flour; slowly stir into sauce. Cook; stir until
thickened. Slowly blend in sour cream; heat.
Serve over cooked noodles.

Steak with Mustard Marinade

1 lb. round steak,
1/4 c. Dijon-style
mustard
1-1/2 Tbsp soy
sauce
1-1/2 Tbsp dry
sherry wine

1 Tbsp brown sugar
1-1/2 tsp vegetable
oil
1 clove garlic,
minced
1/4 tsp Tabasco
pepper sauce

Place steak in large shallow dish or plastic bag. Combine & mix well remaining ingredients & add to steak. Cover & refrigerate at least 5 hours; turn meat occasionally. Remove meat from marinade; place on grill & brush with marinade. Grill 15 minutes; turn meat & brush with marinade. Grill 10 minutes longer or until desired doneness.

Sukiyaki Skillet

1/4 c. Russian dressing
2 tsp soy sauce
2 tsp brown sugar
1/2 lb. boneless sir-
  loin or flank steak,
  cut into thin strips
2 tsp cornstarch
1-1/2 c. combined
  vegetables - can

use any 3 of the
following: sliced
  celery, green
  onions, mush-
  rooms, water
  chestnuts, bam-
  boo shoots, fresh
  spinach, or
  bean sprouts

In shallow baking dish, blend dressing, soy sauce & brown sugar; add beef. Cover & marinate in refrigerator, turning occasionally, at least 2 hours. Remove beef, reserving marinade; toss with cornstarch. In large skillet, over high heat, brown beef. Add combined vegetables & cook, stiring constantly, 2 minutes or until vegetables are tender. Add reserved marinade & heat through. Serve, if desired over rice.

Beef Barbecue

1-1/2 lb. boneless beef chuck roast
1/3 c. apricot-pineapple jam
1 Tbsp soy sauce
1/2 tsp ground ginger
1/2 tsp grated lemon peel

Slice roast across grain into 1/4 inch thick slices. In bowl, combine
remaining ingredients. Grill beef slices on uncovered grill, over
medium-hot charcoal briquets 8-10 minutes. Turn & baste often with
jam mixture.

Pot Roast Supreme

1 beef roast
flour
3 carrots
3 potatoes
1/2 - 1 can French onion soup, heated

Dredge meat in flour on both sides. Brown the roast in oil or shortening. Put roast in baking dish. Add carrots & potatoes. Pour heated soup over all.
Bake, covered, at 275° for 4 hours.

Beef & Noodles

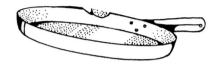

1 can roast beef
1 can water
egg noodles

Combine desired amount of noodles with beef & water.
Cook covered in a skillet about 10 minutes or until noodles are done.

Italian Beef Au Jus

1-1/2 lb. thawed boneless beef roast
1/2 pkg (or 5 oz.) Au Jus Mix
1/2 pkg (or .35 oz.) Italian salad dressing mix
1/2 can (or 5-1/4 oz.) beef broth
1/2 soup can water

Place roast in slow cooker; combine remaining ingredients & pour
over beef. Cover; cook on low for 8 hours. Meat may be sliced &
served with hard rolls or shredded with two forks & served over
noodles or rice, with broth thickened with flour.

Beef Hash

1 Tbsp margarine
1/2 c. cubed cooked
  roast beef
1 medium potato,
  cubed
1 Tbsp onion,
  chopped

2 Tbsp water
1/4 tsp instant
  beef bouillon
  granules
1/8 tsp pepper

Melt margarine in skillet. Add remaining ingredients & mix well.
Cover & cook over low heat until potato is fork-tender, about 10
minutes. Uncover & cook 5 minutes longer.

Grilled Corned Beef 'N Swiss Sandwiches

4 slices bread
1 pkg (3 oz.) thinly sliced corned beef
1-2 Tbsp prepared Thousand Island
 dressing
2 slices Swiss cheese
margarine, softened

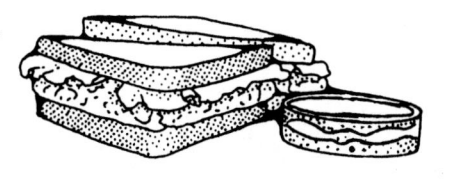

Heat skillet. To assemble sandwiches, place 1/2 of corned beef, 1/2 of dressing & 1 slice cheese between 2 slices of bread. Spread margarine on outside of each sandwich. Grill sandwiches in skillet over medium high heat about 1 minute on each side or until bread is golden brown & cheese is melted. Makes 2 sandwiches.

Bake & Glaze Ribs

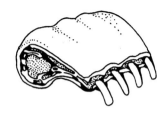

1-1/2 lb. pork spareribs
1/4 tsp garlic powder
1/4 tsp pepper
1/3 c. Teriyaki Baste & Glaze
1/4 tsp grated lemon peel

Cut ribs into serving pieces; place, meaty side up, in shallow foil-lined baking pan. Sprinkle garlic powder & pepper evenly over ribs; cover pan loosely with foil. Bake 45 minutes at 350°. Combine teriyaki baste & lemon peel. Brush both sides of ribs with glaze mixture. Recover & bake 40 minutes longer or until ribs are tender, brushing with glaze mixture occasionally.

Baked Pork Chops

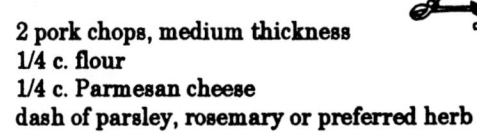

2 pork chops, medium thickness
1/4 c. flour
1/4 c. Parmesan cheese
dash of parsley, rosemary or preferred herb

Salt & pepper chops. Coat chops on both sides in flour & then in
cheese. Put into casserole & add seasonings. Bake at 350° for 1 hour.
Baking time should be decreased for thinner chops.

Italian Pork Chops

1 Tbsp vegetable oil
2 pork chops, 1/2 inch thick
1 c. spaghetti sauce

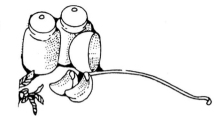

In skillet, cook chops 10 minutes or until browned on both sides. Pour off fat. Add spaghetti sauce & heat to boiling. Reduce heat to low. Cover; cook 5 minutes or until chops are no longer pink.

Smothered Liver & Onions

1 Tbsp margarine
1/2 onion, thinly sliced
1/2 lb. beef liver,
 1/4" thick
1/2 can cream of mush-
 room soup

2 Tbsp milk or
 half & half
dash of pepper

In microwave-safe baking dish, combine margarine & onion. Cover with vented plastic wrap; microwave on High 5 minutes or until onion is tender, stirring once during cooking. Cut liver into 2 portions. Arrange liver over onions, placing thicker portions toward edges of dish. In small bowl, stir soup until smooth; stir in milk & pepper. Pour over liver. Cover, microwave on High 10 minutes or until liver is no longer pink in center, rearranging liver twice during cooking. Let stand, covered, 5 minutes before serving.

Grilled Smoked Sausage

1/3 c. apricot or pineapple preserves
1 tsp lemon juice
1/2 lb. smoked sausage

In small saucepan, heat preserves. Strain; reserve fruit pieces.
Combine strained preserve liquid with lemon juice. Grill whole
sausage on uncovered grill, 5 minutes. Brush with glaze; grill
sausage about 5 minutes longer, turning & brushing with glaze
occasionally. Garnish with fruit pieces.

Ham & Macaroni Toss

1/2 can Cream of
  Chicken soup
2 Tbsp celery, chopped
1 Tbsp onion, chopped
1 Tbsp green pepper,
  chopped
1/2 tsp prepared
  mustard

dash of pepper &
  hot pepper sauce
1 c. cooked
  macaroni
3/4 c. diced
  cooked ham

Combine soup, celery, onion, green pepper, mustard, pepper & hot pepper sauce. Add macaroni & ham. Chill.
Serve with tomato wedges.

Ham & Cheese Dinner

3/4 c. celery, sliced
1 Tbsp margarine
1/2 can Cheddar
  cheese soup
1/2 c. diced cooked
  ham

1/2 of 4 oz. can
  sliced mushrooms,
  drained
1/4 c. milk
4 oz. egg noodles,
  cooked, drained

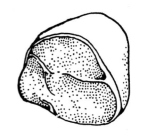

Saute celery in butter in saucepan over medium heat until crisp-tender, about 7 minutes. Stir in soup, ham, mushrooms, milk & mustard. Cook & stir until hot, about 5 minutes. Serve over noodles.

Pizza Bread

1 mini French roll, 8"
  long, sliced length-
  wise
margarine, softened
grated Parmesan
  cheese

2 oz. pizza sauce
1/8 lb. sliced
  pepperoni
sliced Mozzarella
  cheese
dried oregano leaves

Spread margarine over cut sides of roll & sprinkle with Parmesan
cheese. Broil until lightly browned. Spread several tablespoons pizza
sauce over each. Layer pepperoni over sauce. Top with Mozzarella
cheese & sprinkle with oregano.
Broil until cheese melts.

Reuben Sandwich

2 slices turkey
  pastrami
4 slices pumper-
  nickel bread
1 Tbsp 1000 Island
  dressing
1/4 c. drained sauer-
  kraut

2 slices Swiss
  cheese
1/4 onion, chopped
margarine,
  melted

Layer pastrami on bread. Spread with dressing. Top pastrami with 2 Tbsp sauerkraut, 1 Tbsp onion & a slice of cheese. Brush bread with melted margarine. Grill in skillet **until** bread is crisp & cheese is melted.

My Favorite Recipes

Poultry

Oven-Fried Chicken

2 Tbsp margarine	1/8 tsp pepper
1/4 c. flour	1-1/2 lb. chicken
3/4 tsp salt	parts (about 1/2
1/2 tsp paprika	of a chicken)

Heat oven to 425° In oven, melt margarine in baking pan. Put flour &
spices into paper or plastic bag. Shake 2 or 3 chicken pieces at a time in
bag until thoroughly coated. Place skin side down in margarine. Bake
uncovered 30 minutes. Turn chicken & continue baking until tender, 20-
30 minutes longer until chicken is done.

Coat 'N Bake Chicken Wings

1/3 c. fine bread
  crumbs
1/2 tsp onion
  powder
1/2 tsp basil,
  crushed
1/4 tsp garlic salt

1/4 tsp paprika
1-1/2 tsp water
1 egg
1 lb. chicken
  wings, tips
  removed

Heat oven to 425°. Lightly grease cookie sheet. In shallow dish, combine bread crumbs, onion powder, basil, garlic salt, & paprika. In another dish, combine water & egg; beat well. Dip each wing in beaten egg; roll in bread crumb mixture to coat. Place in prepared pan. Bake 15 minutes; turn, bake 15-18 minutes or until chicken is tender & golden brown.

Easy Baked Chicken

1-1/2 lb. chicken pieces
8 oz. Italian dressing
6 oz. apricot preserves

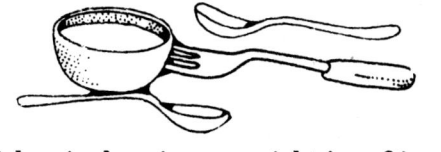

In covered dish, marinate chicken in dressing overnight in refrigerator. Heat oven to 325°. Remove chicken from marinade. In small bowl, combine 1/2 cup marinade with preserves; mix well. Brush chicken with this mixture; place skin-side up in baking dish. Pour marinade over chicken to prevent overbaking. Cover with aluminum foil.
Bake at 325° for 30-40 minutes or until chicken is tender.

Baked Chicken

1/2 pkg. dry onion
  soup mix
1/3 c. dry bread
  crumbs
dash of pepper
1 egg white

1 Tbsp water
2 chicken breast
  halves, skinless
  & boneless
1 Tbsp margarine,
  melted

Combine soup mix, breas crumbs, & pepper. Mix egg & water. Dip
chicken into egg & then coat with crumbs. Drizzle margarine over
chicken. Bake at 400˚ for 20 minutes or until done.

Chicken Italiano
with Zip

1/2 c. mayonnaise
1/3 c. Italian dressing
3-4 pieces chicken

Mix ingredients together & pour over chicken.
Grill or broil until chicken is done.

Baked Chicken Breast

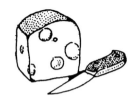

1-2 chicken breast halves, skinned & deboned
2-3 slices Swiss cheese
1/2 can Cream of Mushroom soup

1/8 c. white wine
1/2 - 1 c. crushed croutons
1/8 c. melted butter (2 Tbsp)

Arrange chicken in baking dish. Lay slice of cheese over each chicken breast. Combine soup with wine & pour over chicken. Top with croutons. Drizzle butter over all.
Bake 350° for 3/4 - 1 hour.

Baked Apricot Chicken

5 oz. apricot or peach
  preserves
2 Tbsp lemon juice
1 tsp soy sauce
1/4 tsp salt

1-1/2 lb. chicken pieces
1/2 c. dry bread
  crumbs
2 Tbsp margarine,
  melted

In shallow dish, combine preserves, lemon juice, soy sauce & salt. Coat chicken with apricot mixture; roll in bread crumbs. Set aside remaining apricot mixture. In greased baking dish, arrange chicken; drizzle with margarine. Bake uncovered at 350° for 1 hour or until tender. Heat remaining apricot mixture.
Serve with chicken.

Plum Good Chicken

Chicken pieces 1/4 c. orange juice
1/2 c. soy sauce 1 clove garlic,
1/2 c. plum jam   crushed
1/4 c. honey

Mix ingredients, except chicken, to make sauce. Place chicken in baking dish, skin side down. Brush with sauce & pour rest of sauce over chicken. Cover & bake at 325° for 30 minutes. Baste & turn chicken over.
Bake, uncovered, for 30 minutes more. Serve with sauce from pan.

Lemon-Glazed Chicken

1-1/2 lb. chicken pieces,
  skinned
1/2 tsp salt
1/8 tsp pepper
3 oz. grozen lemonade concentrate,
  thawed
1-1/2 tsp soy sauce

Sprinkle chicken with salt & pepper; place chicken in shallow baking dish. Mix concentrate & soy sauce; pour over chicken. Bake 40 minutes at 400°, turning chicken over once & basting occasionally. Bake until chicken is browned & fork-tender.

Chicken Rose

2 chicken breasts,
   skinned (3-4 oz. each)
2 Tbsp rose wine
2 Tbsp soy sauce
1-1/2 tsp oil

1 Tbsp water
1/2 tsp ginger
1/2 tsp oregano
1-1/2 tsp brown
   sugar

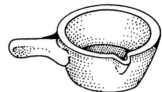

Place chicken breasts in baking dish. Make sauce by combining
remaining ingredients. Pour sauce over chicken & sprinkle lightly
with garlic powder.
Cover & bake for 1-1/2 hours at 375°

Turkey Parmesan

1 tsp margarine
1 slice (1 oz) raw
  turkey breast
1-1/2 Tbsp spaghetti
  sauce

1/2 tsp grated
  Parmesan cheese
1/2-1 slice Moz-
  zarella process
  cheese

In skillet, over medium heat, melt margarine. Add turkey slice. Cook 2 minutes; turn. Reduce heat to low; top turkey with remaining ingredients. Cover; cook 2-3 minutes longer.

Delicious Stir-Fry

1/2 chicken breast, skinned & boned
1/2 lb. fresh broccoli
1 Tbsp vegetable oil
1/2 onion, chunked
1 Tbsp water

1 green or red Bell pepper, chunked
1/4 lb. fresh mushrooms, quartered
1/4 c. Stir-Fry sauce

Cut chicken into 1 inch square pieces. Remove flowerets from broccoli; cut into bite-size pieces. Peel stalks, cut into thin slices. Heat oil in hot wok or skillet over high heat. Add chicken; stir-fry 1 minute. Add broccoli & onion; stir-fry 1 minute. Add water; cover & cook 2 minutes, stirring once. Add pepper & mushrooms; stir-fry 2 minutes. Stir in stir-fry sauce. Cook & stir until chicken & vegetables are coated with sauce. Serve immediately. Can serve over rice.

Stir-Fried Chicken Fajitas

2 boneless, skinned chicken breast halves, cut in thin strips
1/3 c. bottled Italian dressing
1/2 onion, sliced, separated into rings
1/2 green pepper, sliced in strips
1/2 red pepper, sliced in strips
1/2 c. sliced fresh mushrooms (can use canned)
1/4 tsp garlic salt
1 Tbsp lemon juice
salt & pepper to taste
flour tortillas
Picante sauce/sour cream

In heavy plastic bag, combine chicken strips & dressing; refrigerate for several hours or overnight, turning bag occasionally. Drain. Heat a 12 inch non-stick skillet over medium high heat; stir-fry chicken strips & onions for 2 minutes. Add pepper strips & mushrooms; cook & stir until chicken is done & peppers are tender-crisp. Season with garlic salt, lemon juice & salt & pepper. Serve in warm tortillas. Top with Picante sauce & sour cream.

Easy Chicken Enchiladas

1 can chunk chicken
1 c. Cheddar cheese, shredded
2 oz. chopped green chilies, drained (optional)
2 Tbsp onion, chopped
5 oz. enchilada sauce

4 corn tortillas (6")
optional toppings:
shredded lettuce
sour cream
diced tomatoes

In bowl, combine chicken, 1/2 c. cheese, chilies, & onion. In a baking dish, spread half of the enchilada sauce. Spread 1/4 c. chicken mixture in each tortilla & roll up, placing seam-side down in sauce in the baking dish. Pour remaining enchilada sauce over the enchiladas & sprinkle the remaining cheese over the top of enchiladas. Cover; bake at 350˚ for 25 minutes. Top with lettuce, sour cream and tomatoes.

Turkey-Broccoli Melt

8 oz. frozen broccoli
  spears
2 tsp prepared
  mustard
2 slices bread, toasted
  (preferably whole
  wheat)
2 (1 oz. ea.) slices
  turkey breast

2 Tbsp shredded
  sharp Cheddar
  cheese
1/2 c. alfalfa
  sprouts
  (optional)

Cook broccoli according to package directions. Drain; set aside.
Spread 1 teaspoon mustard over each bread slice; place on a baking
sheet. Top each with 1 turkey slice, broccoli & 1 tablespoon cheese.
Broil 3 inches from heat for 1-1/2 minutes. Top with 1/4 cup sprouts.
Serve immediately.

Creamed Turkey Stack-Ups

1 c. cubed cooked
  turkey or chicken
2 Tbsp margarine
2 Tbsp flour
1 c. milk
1-1/2 tsp instant
  chicken bouillon
  granuels

1-1/2 oz. sliced
  mushrooms,
  drained
2 Tbsp green
  pepper, chopped
1 oz. sliced
  pimientos,
drained pancakes (4-6)

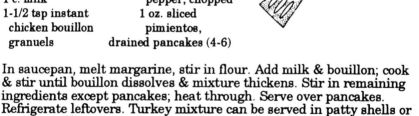

In saucepan, melt margarine, stir in flour. Add milk & bouillon; cook & stir until bouillon dissolves & mixture thickens. Stir in remaining ingredients except pancakes; heat through. Serve over pancakes. Refrigerate leftovers. Turkey mixture can be served in patty shells or as a crepe filling.

95

Chicken Casserole

3/4 c. chicken,
  cooked & diced
1/2 c. macaroni,
  uncooked
1/2 can cream of celery
  soup
1/2 can chicken broth
2 Tbsp onion, chopped

1/4 c. cubed
  processed cheese
1/8 tsp salt
1/8 tsp pepper
bread crumbs
  for topping

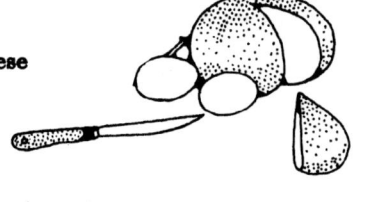

Mix all ingredients (except for bread crumbs) & place in 8"x8" pan. Place in refrigerator overnight (covered). Bake at 350° for 1 hour (45 minutes covered & 15 minutes uncovered).
Top with bread crumbs. Bake 15 minutes more.

Scalloped Turkey

1/2 c. cooked turkey, sliced
1/8 lb. processed cheese
1/2 c. chicken broth
1/4 c. onion, chopped
1/2 c. uncooked macaroni
1 hard-boiled egg
1/2 can cream of celery soup
1/2 can (4 oz.) sliced water chestnuts
salt & pepper to taste

Mix all ingredients together & refrigerate overnight in a baking dish. Bake at 325° for 1-1/2 hours.

Turkey Stroganoff

2 Tbsp green pepper,
diced
2 Tbsp onion,
chopped
1 Tbsp margarine
1/2 can cream of
mushroom soup

1/4 c. sour cream
1 c. cooked noodles
3/4 c. cubed,
cooked turkey
1/4 tsp paprika

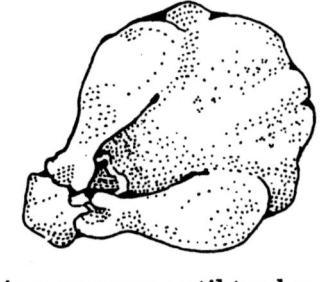

In saucepan, cook green pepper & onion in margarine until tender.
In 1 qt. casserole, blend soup & sour cream. Stir in remaining
ingredients. Bake at 350° for 35 minutes or until hot; stir. Sprinkle
with additional paprika.

Chicken Stroganoff

2 Tbsp margarine
1/2 lb. chicken breasts, cut into strips
1 c. fresh mushrooms, sliced
1/4 c. onion, chopped
1/2 can cream of chicken soup
1/4 c. sour cream
2 c. egg noodles, cooked & drained

Brown chicken in half of margarine in a skillet; remove. Add remaining margarine & cook mushrooms & onion until tender. Stir in soup & sour cream. Heat to boiling & add chicken & heat. Serve over hot, cooked noodles.

Quick Chicken Dinner

5 oz. frozen mixed
   vegetables
1/2 can cream of
   chicken soup
2 oz. mushroom stems
   & pieces, undrained

1/4 c. onion,
   chopped
3/4 c. cut-up cooked
   chicken
1/2 c. crushed
   potato chips

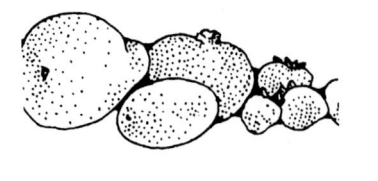

Rinse frozen vegetables with cold water to separate; drain. Mix
vegetables, soup, mushrooms, & onion in a saucepan. Heat to boiling;
reduce heat. Cover & simmer 8-10 minutes, stirring occasionally, until
vegetables are done. Stir in chicken; heat until hot.
Sprinkle with potato chips. Serve over toast or biscuits if desired.

Turkey Tetrazzini

1/2 can cream of mush-
  room soup
1/4 c. milk
1/4 c. onion, chopped
2 Tbsp Parmesan
  cheese
1/4 c. sour cream
1 c. cooked turkey
  or chicken

1/2 c. zucchini, cut
  in half lengthwise
  & thinly sliced
1 c. cooked
  spaghetti
  (2 oz. dry)

Combine all ingredients & bake at 375° for 30 minutes or until hot &
bubbly.

Polynesian Chicken Salad

1/4 c. Russian or garlic French dressing
1 c. cut-up cooked chicken
1/2 c. cooked rice
1/2 c. sliced celery
1/2 can pineapple chunks, drained (about 6 oz.)
1/2 c. seedless grapes
1/4 tsp salt
1/4 tsp curry powder
1/8 tsp ginger

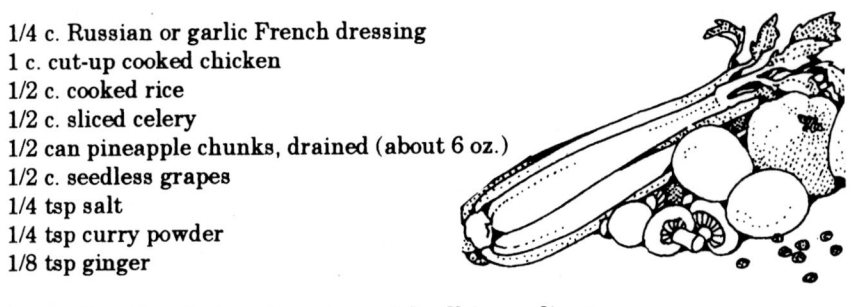

In medium bowl, toss dressing with all ingredients
Chill at least 1 hour. Arrange in lettuce cups.

Hot Chicken Salad

2/3 c. cooked chicken, chopped
1/2 c. celery, chopped
1/2 c. cheese, grated
1/4 c. mayonnaise

1 tsp lemon juice
2/3 c. potato chips, crushed-divided
1 Tbsp margarine, melted

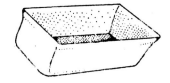

Mix first 5 ingredients, salt & pepper to taste & 1/3 c. potato chips. Place in 1 quart baking dish. Combine 1/3 c. potato chips & melted margarine, drizzle over top of chicken mixture.
Bake at 350° for 30 minutes.

Chicken Broccoli Dish

1/2 lb. fresh broccoli, cut (or 5 oz. frozen broccoli spears)
1 c. cooked chicken, diced
1/2 can cream of broccoli soup

1/4 c. milk
1/4 c. Cheddar cheese, shredded
2 Tbsp dry bread crumbs
1 Tbsp margarine, melted

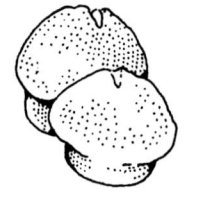

Put broccoli & chicken in baking dish. In a bowl, combine the soup & milk; pour over broccoli & chicken. Sprinkle cheese over top. Combine bread crumbs & margarine & sprinkle over the cheese. Bake at 450° for 20 minutes.

Seafood

Marinated Fish

4 fish fillets (from 2 fish)
Italian dressing
Margarine

Marinate fish in Italian dressing for 1 hour, using enough dressing to
cover fish. Place fish in foil with a few tablespoons of margarine & a
little marinade. Broil or grill until done (when fish flakes with a
fork); or bake on a cookie sheet at 375° for 35 minutes.

Fish Fillets Au Gratin

1/2 lb. fish fillets
1-1/2 tsp lemon juice
1/2 tsp chopped fresh
   parsley
1/4 tsp onion salt

1/4 tsp paprika
dash pepper
1/4 c. shredded
   shredded
American cheese

Place fish fillets in baking dish. Sprinkle with remaining ingredients, except cheese. Bake at 350° for 15-20 minutes or until fish flakes easily with fork. Sprinkle cheese over fish during last 3 minutes of baking time. _Microwave directions_: Cover dish with plastic wrap & microwave on High for 7-9 minutes or until fish flakes easily with fork, rearranging fish once halfway through ooking. Remove cover; drain well. Sprinkle with cheese; microwave on High for 45-60 seconds or until cheese is melted.

Green Bean & Fish Casserole

1/4 c. onion, chopped
1 Tbsp margarine
1/4 c. dry white wine
  or chicken broth
16 oz. can French-style
  green beans, drained
1/2 can cream of mush-
  room soup

2 oz. mushroom
  stems & pieces,
  drained
1/2 of a 2.8 oz. can
  French fried
  onions
6 oz. crunchy
  frozen fish fillets

Heat oven to 400°. Grease baking dish. Cook onion in margarine in a saucepan over medium heat, stirring frequently, until tender. Stir in wine, beans, soup, & mushrooms; heat through. Pour into baking dish. Top with French fried onions or until mixture is bubbly & fillets are hot.

Scallops with Golden Cream Sauce

1 Tbsp margarine
1/2 red pepper, cut
 into thin strips
1/2 c. uncooked
 regular rice
1/2 envelope dry Golden
 Onion Recipe soup mix

1 c. water
1/2 Tbsp lime juice
2 Tbsp light cream
 or half & half
1/2 lb. bay scallops
1 green onion,
 sliced

In medium skillet, melt margarine & cook red pepper until crisp-tencer. Stir in rice, then dry soup mix that has been blended with water & lime juice. Bring to a boil, then simmer covered 30 minutes or until rice is tender. Stir in remaining ingredients & cook covered 5 minutes or until scallops are tender. Serve, if desired, with freshly ground pepper.

Seafood Salad Sandwiches

1/2 envelope dry
  vegetable recipe
  soup mix
1/3 c. sour cream
2 Tbsp mayonnaise
1/2 tsp lemon juice
1/4 c. chopped celery

hot pepper sauce
  to taste
  (optional)
dash pepper
1 (6 oz.) pkg. frozen
  crabmeat, thawed
  & well-drained*

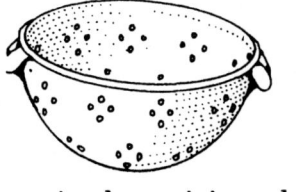

In bowl, blend soup mix, sour cream, mayonnaise, lemon juice, celery, hot pepper sauce & pepper. Stir in crabmeat; chill. To serve, line rolls with lettuce and fill with crab mixture.

Variations: Use 6 oz. frozen pre-cooked shrimp coarsely chopped; or 1 can tuna, drained & flaked; or 1 can (4-1/2 oz.) shrimp, drained & chopped; or 1 can (6-1/2 oz.) crabmeat, drained & flaked.